BX9178 .S64 O4

I0818956

THE OLD IN THE NEW;

OR,

The Position and Policy of the Presbyterian Church

IN THE UNITED STATES;

A DISCOURSE,

DELIVERED AT THE

OPENING OF THE GENERAL ASSEMBLY,

IN ST. LOUIS, MAY 17, 1855,

BY THOMAS H. SKINNER, D. D.,

PROFESSOR OF SACRED RHETORIC, PASTORAL THEOLOGY AND CHURCH POLITY IN THE UNION THEOLOGICAL SEMINARY.

SAINT LOUIS:

KEITH, WOODS & CO., PRINTERS.

1855.

BX
9178
.S64
O4

gift
Tappan Presb. Assoc.
3-27-1933

St. Louis, May 21, 1855.

Rev. T. H. Skinner, D. D.:

Dear Sir: The undersigned having listened with great pleasure to the opening sermon of the present session of the General Assembly, delivered by you, and regarding it as a pre-eminently wise and apposite exposition of the denominational and theological position and duties of our church, the general circulation of which would be adapted to foster a heathful interest in our body, take the liberty to request of you a copy for publication.

JAMES P. WILLSON,
HENRY A. ROWLAND,
A. BULLARD,
HENRY NEILL,
C. R. ROBERT,
HENRY B. SMITH,
WM. C. WISNER.

St. Louis, May 22, 1855.

The Rev. James P. Willson, D. D., and others:

Dear Brethren: In compliance with your request I give you my discourse for publication, although it was not designed for the press, and I fear is not altogether suited for it.

Yours, with great regard,
THOMAS H. SKINNER.

DISCOURSE.

I WRITE NO NEW COMMANDMENT UNTO YOU, BUT AN OLD COMMANDMENT, WHICH YE HAD FROM THE BEGINNING. AGAIN, A NEW COMMANDMENT I WRITE UNTO YOU.—1 *John ii*, 7, 8.

It is common, in popular discourse, to contradict our own assertions immediately after making them—to say what we go on to deny, or deny what we have just said. We do not, however, in such cases, either intend to be inconsistent with ourselves, or speak inadvertently; our design is to set the thing we speak of into contrast with itself, under different aspects. We speak of the thing in the second instance, in a different relation, or with a different reference from that which we intended in the first. The apostle, in our text, does not mean to contradict himself, when, after saying, "I write no new commandment," he adds, in the following sentence, "Again, a new commandment I write." What he wrote was, for substance, "the word which the church had had from the beginning." It was, therefore, nothing new. But yet it was new, in a sense, on account of the new light which was shining in respect to it; the new associations and enforcements it had received—the fullness of meaning which it had been shown to contain.

There has been but one true religion. There are two Testaments; but the religion they contain is one. Christianity, the new commandment of the apostle, is but the faith of the antedeluvian elders, in its maturity and completeness. The books of the New Testament, in their historical, doctrinal, and ethical details, and in their diversified style, diction, examples, illustrations, are but the perfect edition of a religion, the rudiments of which were given to man by his Maker, near the beginning of his existence: regarding it in its date, it was old, regarding it in the stage of development which it had reached, it was strangely new: eye had not seen, ear had not heard it; the thought of it had not entered into the heart of man.

The apostle might speak of it as new, comparing it with itself, under the latest of its antecedent forms; those not only of the last of the prophets, and of the harbinger of our Lord, but of our

Lord himself, previous to his ascension. Even during his personal ministry, there was scarcely the twilight of evangelical truth, when compared with the full-day brightness with which it shone after the baptism of the Holy Ghost and of fire.

Nor have the epithets old and new ceased to be applicable to Christianity. There has been progress in the knowledge of Christianity—progress from vagueness to precision, from obscurity to splendor, in some points—since the days of the apostles. There have been no authentic additions to it; but new representations and impressions have been given of it, from time to time, in virtue of which it has been itself called new. At different epochs, it has become almost as new as it was at first, in its new manifestations of power, and in the new impressions which men have had of it. It was so in the early part of the sixteenth century, when its republication by the reformers, was as a resurrection of it to the nations of Europe. Indeed, at every period of awakening in the church, the ancient faith becomes new again. Nay, it is, as it were, constantly rejuvenizing itself in the experience of individual Christians, to many of whom it seems to be always becoming more and more novel. The old, primitive word, the same essentially, yesterday, to-day and forever, appears to them each day more fresh than when it first opened itself to them. It is always recognized by them as the same old commandment, but it has a new aspect; everything in it looks perfectly fresh and young; its facts, teachings, tendencies, bearings, relations, influences, are ever and more and more new.

This power of self-rejuvenescence, this old-new, or new-old life of our religion, is what makes it a religion for all time—for universal man, till the end of the world. It would not otherwise have a permanently saving power. It does not possess this power, as being simply historic, that is to say, not a myth or fabulous, but founded in fact; this is necessary, but not sufficient: to meet the wants of man in successive generations, Christianity must be unlike other religions in two respects—not only in having a ground, as they have not, in veritable history, but also in having power to renovate and reproduce its ground, so as to make it no less real and manifest to others of the remotest times, than it was to those who lived in the beginning. The past must return in the present; antiquity must reappear in novelty: a merely historic religion is not an available one—does not, cannot answer the purpose of religion. Dying man needs a Saviour, and one inhabiting the present equally with the past, and one, moreover, present to him, and with him, as he walks through the valley of the shadow of death, more really, more perfectly, than any fellow-mortal can be at any time. The ability of the Christian history, of the ground-fact of Christianity, to reproduce itself in the present, to be always fresh, young, palpable, as at first, in the experience of believers, is, in truth, its saving ability. Christianity, divine in its essence—a divine life, as well as a divine doctrine—having its spring in God—and being vitalized and sustained by the indwelling spirit of God—being, moreover, not only historic, but the key of history—its Author being the Creator and Ruler of the world, who orders the events of time with reference to its advancement, and to the same end exerts, when He pleases, supernatural forces: Hence its permanent efficiency as a religion for man; its antiquity and also its perpetual and progressive novelty, its venerable age, and also its eternal youth and freshness.

This two-fold characteristic of Christianity has given rise to a principle of classification and division in the church. The epithets *old* and *new*, from this, as the occasion, have been applied to different classes of Christians. Among Christians, as among men, some are constitutionally conservative, some versatile and impulsive: hence antagonisms, "sides," "schools," "lights,"—one called *old* from their attachment to the oldness, the antiquity of Christianity; the other *new*, from their characteristic susceptibility to the power of the novelty in which Christianity arrays itself from time to time.

The latter designation has been applied to the church before whose representative assembly I am speaking. They have not taken it to themselves; it has been given to them, from what motive, I say not; perhaps it was that which first suggested "Christians" as an appropriate name for the disciples of our Lord: but understanding it in a good sense—a sense which it will bear—we need not, I think, be reluctant to be called by it. So taken, it imports no comparison of old and new in Christianity itself, no ground or possibility of a difference between Christianity at first and afterwards, but only a special liveliness or impressibility to new manifestations of what is, in inself, old. This implies no want of interest or delight in the old faith—it is, in truth, this delight, this interest itself. The novelty, whose power is felt, is not absolute novelty; it is antiquity in novelty; the new does but reproduce the old; it is the same old Christianity which the apostles preached, giving new proofs of its identity, and of its invincible, undying, ever-efficient power to save.—It is not a reproach, it is not weakness, to be perfectly alive, to novelty, under this idea of it. It is honorable to be called new for such a reason, and more so than old, if the latter term is to be understood in a sense implying that the other is not honorable.

I have thought, fathers and brethren, that it will not be a misapplication of our time, on this occasion, if we employ what remains of it in considering our own interest as a church—what especially concerns us as having, under the providence of God, a distinctive denominational existence, and, doubtless, a distinctive and not unimportant mission to fulfil, in our day and country. Our position and circumstances have suggested this as an opportune subject. We are manifestly in a transition state—emerging out of what has been regarded as a precarious condition, into one of more stability. Placed between, and, in some vital respects, mingled with two large religious bodies, to one of which one part of us, to the other another part had strong affinity, our absorption into them has been anticipated and predicted: there is no longer hope or apprehension of this. A lively preference of our order, a high appreciation of its specific advantages, has developed itself amongst us, under circumstances specially suited to foster and extend it. Possibly, we are in some danger from a too active, too impulsive denominationalism. We are, at least, not without temptations to excess. Is it not wise to look to ourselves, lest the perils with which we are threatened come upon us? How desirable that our movements as a church be now specially marked by discretion, by soundness of judgment, by the fear of God, by the meekness of heavenly wisdom, and be under the direction of the Spirit of God. Thus, only thus, may we earnestly and safely pursue *the means of our denominational success*, to the consideration of which I have ventured to ask your attention.

The points which seem to me most deserving of our thought, are the following: To guard against excessive denominationalism; to regulate the exercise of the principle, the propensity, which in one way or another, has occasioned our distinct denominational existence and name; to increase our corporate strength; to adapt our activity to its appointed sphere and times; and, in our administrative measures, to give a higher regard to the end for which the church was designed, than has been common in any church.

I. To guard against excess in denominational activity, I assume the legitimateness, the expediency even, of denominationalism, diversity of order and form in the church. It has no necessary connection with sectarianism: that is the bane of Christianity, but denominationalism, apart from the spirit of sect, is but diversity in unity, which, in the scheme of the world and in Deity itself, is the condition of perfection. Within the pale of the church, denominationalism, or its equivalent, is inevitable and indispensable, unless no regard is to be had to variety of circumstances—that is to say, unless practical wisdom and even common sense should be renounced in the organization and discipline of churches. If it be insisted, that the different churches, with their diversities of form, might be subject to the same ecclesiastical rule, this, supposing the diversities to be adequate, would be precisely the same, with unsectarian denominationalism, and the controversy would be about only a name. It is not, therefore, schismatical, or, in any respect, unchristian, for a company of Christians, under certain circumstances and within certain limits, to prefer a peculiar church order: simply denominational organizations are warrantable, doubtless, from the New Testament; are, in principle, if not in practice, apostolical; are organizations in behalf of simple catholic Christianity, fittingly arrayed as to externals by the influence of circumstances and accidents. They are not only allowable, they are necessary—necessary to the highest triumph and the speediest progress, if not to the purity and permanence of Christianity. Denominationalism, nevertheless, is peculiarly liable to abuse: there is, perhaps, no extant church which is not more or less an example of this abuse—not one which is not more or less sectarian. Has not the spirit of sect, not mere preference as to form, but an exclusive, unchurching, uncharitable narrowness, given origin to more than one of existing denominations? In organizing themselves, have they not erected mere matters of ceremony, or modes of order, external forms, into walls of separation, barriers to communion, among the members of the body of Christ? In planting churches, in measures for extending themselves, in administrative proceedings, to what extent have they assumed practically, if not theoretically, that other churches of Christ, even the best of these churches, were not his churches—disregarding their preoccupation of places—taking positions with reference to proselytism from them, and either refusing offices of brotherhood, or performing them with sectarian views? There is no spirit, in the exercise of which our moderation, our temperance, our vigilance, should be more exemplary, than in that which inclines us to denominational movements. The desire to be first is often stronger in corporations than in individuals, and in religious corporations, where it is most out of place, it is apt to be stronger than elsewhere; and when this desire can disguise itself under the show of zeal for purity and more effective working, as it always seeks to do in its religious developments, it will suffer no restraint, set itself no limits, suspect itself of nothing amiss, though as craving, as unscrupulous, and as boundless in its ambition as anti-christ himself.

I cannot, therefore, allow myself to stimulate our denominationalism, without endeavoring to secure its activity against the self-deceptive, self-blinding influence of the sectarian spirit, the veritable anti-christ. It is, I doubt not, good, nay, even the best, and may be the instrument of good; it ought not to be inert; its vigorous activity is the condition of our highest efficiency as a church; and, hitherto, since the unhappy dismemberment of the Presbyterian body in this country, it has not been energetic enough amongst us. We seem to have been but feebly tempted by the desire of denominational aggrandizement; we have done too little, given too little thought to our furtherance as a church; we have, perhaps, been excessively inclined to a confraternal, co-operative type of activity, more to others' advancement than our own. It is time, doubtless, to awake out of our sleep, to redeem the time in which we have been so delinquent in duty to ourselves. But let us not forget the peril to Christianity, the general cause of our own and all churches, in so far as our activity is to have its spring, in the desire of advancing our distinctive denominational interest. However legitimate or worthy this motive, there is nothing that acts in this world amidst greater incidental peril to the purpose for which it should act, than the denominational spirit. What danger, that it will cease to be merely denominational? that it will become piously sectarian, piously ambitious, piously manouvering, piously fraudulent? that instead of being a means of advancing the cause of Christ, it will become its own end, and push its own interests against those of other and all denominations; assuming the superiority of a part to the whole, the circumstantial to the essential, the variable to the permanent, making Christians to be exscinders of one another, and Christ to be divided against himself; in a word, substituting the concision, in place of the circumcision.

Perhaps, moreover, we have a special reason for caution. If we are in a transitional state—if we are passing out of an extreme, that of indifference as to our denominational standing, may we not very naturally proceed to the opposite extreme; may not the swing of the pendulum, in this case, be too forcible; may we not advance too fast, and go farther than we should, unless we are careful as to our movement? May we not part sooner than it is expedient to do, with what has hitherto been our distinction—no dishonorable one—that of a comprehensive and co-operative type of activity? Should we not wish to retain this distinction, as far as we can do so, with just self-respect and decorum? Amidst our measures for compacting and enlarging ourselves, which, I am persuaded, should not be as inefficient, as unsystematized, as few, as they have been, should not this one endeavor surmount and overrule every other, namely, to maintain the unity of the spirit in the bonds of peace, in the Universal Church—the common cause and honor of all evangelical denominations? How melancholy a change in us, if our fellowship with the communion of all saints should deny or discredit itself, by refusing to interchange appropriate offices of fellowship with any portion of that blessed and only true communion; if in advancing ourselves into denominational magnitude and strength, we should make our church, not an example and a model, but a shame and a scandal to other churches, and the world?

II. The next point is the regulation of the principle of our denominationalism—that susceptibility to the novel in the manifestations of Christianity which has occasioned our distinctive existence and title. This susceptibility, I repeat, we need not wish to disown. If it be true, that while other religions are becoming antiquated, decrepit, effete, Christianity abides young and fresh as at first, and is always to be giving new manifestations of its immortal vigor, there ought to be some to recognize it in these fresh displays of itself; and if we are quick to do this, it is certainly no disparagement to us—nothing to incur reproach or contempt from our brethren. If Christianity have indeed the character we have ascribed to it, and if its course is to be parallel to that of knowledge, art, civilization; or if the future is to be judged of from the past; or if the prophecies have not been misinterpreted, and the hopes and prayers of the church are to be fulfilled, there is doubtless to be no abatement in the demand for the exercise of New Schoolism; the only question is, whether the demand is to be met, or whether Christianity, in its coming revelations of power and glory, is to be ignored or disowned? The Old School, so called, has one seeming advantage: the true faith is old, and so far as this is concerned, the true school must be an old one, and all questions, as to the claims of schools, are to be settled by referring them to the primitive standards of truth: "Thus saith the Lord, Stand ye in the ways and see, and ask for the old paths." (Jer. 6: 16); but in regard to this, the New School concedes no superiority to the other. We have expressed the sense in which it submits to be called new; and if it is reproached on this account, its reproach reverts at last to those from whom it comes. There is an Old Schoolism with which no connection is to be desired—that which will acknowledge nothing save error and fanaticism in any form of novelty, though from Christianity itself. This, call it what you will, is essentially the same with that ancient traditionalism, that Jews' religion, which stoned the holy prophets and crucified the Lord of glory. There is, we must admit, liability to abuse in the principle of the New School; but there is liability to this, also, on the other side. If, in the way of warning, the latter can point the New School to extravagancies, fanatical excitements, sects, heresies, secessions, this, in return, can remind the Old how often the words of the prophet have been fulfilled in those who have made their boast in venerable antiquity: "Behold ye despisers, and wonder and perish; for I work a work in your days, a work which you shall in nowise believe, though a man declare it unto you." There is probably as much danger of the abuse of principle in the one sbhool as in the other. We recognise certainly no special disadvantage, no inferiority of excellence or value, in the principle of our denominationalism. We give it the preference before every other.

But excellent and noble as it is, there may be need of caution and vigilance as to its exercise. Perhaps it were well for it to be combined with the antagonistic principle. The two schools, as to their influence on each other, perhaps, ought not to be disparted. The development of their respective tendencies might be purer, safer, and at the same time more effective and fruitful, from their conjunct reciprocal action on each other. The new might gain, in one respect, at least, from union with the old: our tendency is to be eager and progressive; theirs conservative; both are needful; each needs to be balanced and corrected by the other. There may be excess in conservatism; at remarkable manifestations of the Spirit, its devotion to antiquity has sometimes restrained it from full sympathy with the new aspects and advances of the truth. There is also, let us admit, an inclination to excess in the activity of the other principle—the susceptibility to the novel—the principle of progress. Novelty may be welcome, not as a new phase or exhibition of the ancient faith, but for its own sake, or as absolute novelty. Pleasure in novelty, simply as such, is sometimes a predominant passion, so intense and active, that the subjects of it spend their time in nothing else but either to tell or hear some new thing. The great adversary of the truth depends, for his success against it, chiefly on his ability to satisfy and actuate this propensity. How vast the multitude and variety of "lying wonders," the food provided by him for the love of novelty in religion, with which the world, and especially this age, is kept so full!

And the actual state of mind in the church in respect of the former belief—the old commandment heard from the beginning, is a startling commentary on the remark now made. "There is," says one of the first of living authors, "there is little, perhaps, in the cycle of our predecessors' confession of faith, which, if challenged to relinquish, we should want to see erased. But whether we be distinctly conscious of the fact or not, there has come to stand over against each article of that belief, a counterbalance, an influence of abatement, an unadjusted surmise, an adverse feeling, neither assented to nor dismissed, but which holds the mind in perpetual suspense. The creed of this time is, let us say, word for word, the creed of sixty years ago; but, if such a simile might be allowed, these *items* of our "confession," now fill one side of a balance-sheet, on the other side of which there stands a heavy charge which has not yet been ascertained or agreed to." Is it a predisposition to novelty or aversion to orthodoxy, to "the old commandment," which is revealing itself, in this misgiving as to the doctrines of the church in other days?

Fathers and brethren, while we rejoice in our denominational independence of tradition, our openness to new manifestations of the truth, let us not forget its temptations—let us rejoice in it with trembling. As far from us as from any others be the absurdity that substantive Christianity has not been understood, that the creed of the church has not yet expressed, for substance, the meaning of Scripture. A faith which is not historic, the roots of which do not strike quite through the past, even to the beginning, the roots, trunk, or branches of which belong to a tree which has been planted since the apostolic age, is not a saving faith, is a tree which has not been planted by our Heavenly Father, and is therefore destined to be rooted up. The apostle intended to make this assertion virtually, when he disclaimed writing "a new commandment." Any writing purporting to embody the gospel, would not be true, it would be onother gospel, if it were absolutely novel: even over the signature of John, or Paul, or an angel from heaven, it would not be worthy of our acceptation. No, in the true faith, that once delivered to the saints, there never is absolute novelty, there is absolute continuity, as unbroken as the course of the ages. That faith may be as a river which widens and deepens, and moves with increasing force, as it advances towards the ocean, but it is ever the same, and the ark, the only ark of salvation, is borne on its current. We do not admit, in saying this, the infallibility of the church, or its perfect knowledge of the Scriptures, nor do we question the right or the duty of each individual to interpret the Scriptures for himself. We are to search the Scriptures; we are to try by them every doctrine, every spirit, every church; we are to call no man, or company of men, master; we are to take as our motto: "Let God be true, but every man a liar." Faith is not credulity; we cannot truly believe, except from sufficient evidence, apparent and satisfactory to ourselves: nevertheless, if what we do believe is absolute novelty, or different, as to substance, from what the church has believed from the beginning; if our interpretation of the Scriptures be essentially different from that of our predecessors, if we have forsaken the "old paths" of former believers, whether as to faith or practice, we have abused our liberty, we have misunderstood or rejected the meaning of the Scriptures; a deceived heart hath turned us aside, and we are as wandering stars, to whom the mist of darkness is reserved.

I have no suspicion that we, as a church, have any special proneness to aberration from the ancient faith. We have given no occasion for this suspicion. Up to this day, our love of the new in religion, has given no proof that it is aught more or less than the love of the old in the new; not disloyalty, but fealty to orthodoxy, has hitherto been as much our distinction as that of the Old School. We may have been freer than they as to our modes of thought and speech, we have had differences from them as to certain points of doctrine, but we have not been less constant to the harmony of the Protestant confessions, and especially to the Westminster confession, our own, and, we think, much the best of them all. We have of late given special evidence of our orthodoxal soundness and firmness. Previous to the disruption of our church it was charged that we were restrained from heretical outbreaks by ecclesiastical connections; but since that sad event, we have not declined in our orthodoxy; we have stood firm and united on our old doctrinal basis; and this amidst a revival of outside errors and delusions, by which, had it been possible, the very elect might have been carried away. To God be praise, for this testimonial of our loyalty to his truth. It cannot, without uncharitableness be discarded or gainsayed; nevertheless, let us not deny that our active, progressive tendency has not been without a snare; and that it is to the effectual grace of God that our steadfastness is to be ascribed. Let us also keep ourselves apprised of the circumstances of peculiar temptation which still beset us; and finally, let us admit, that in our isolation from our brethren, we have more cause to be on our guard against excess in the exercise of our denominational principle, more need of self-supervision and self-control in respect to it, than when we were more subject to their conservative oversight.

III. Under the hedge of restrictions and cautions which I have placed about the subject, I may now urge, thirdly, the giving of proper care in order to nourish and develope our corporate strength. I speak of strength purely denominational, not in any form or degree sectarian, strength to be used for our own purposes, only in so far as they involve the common cause of Christians, the ultimate end for which the church exists. In this view it is an object of desire, and the acquisition and exertion of it, a duty as far as in us lies.

But here, doubtless, it is at once felt that a special obstacle is to be encountered in the principle of our denominationalism. This principle, that of the highest freedom, of ready fealty to truth whether in an old or a new aspect, has little affinity for any forecasted apparatus or machinery of church action; the only frame work it would choose to put itself in, is that of spontaneous growth, the upspring of its own free unforced dynamic life. It is especially reluctant to engage in the ordinary means of denominational consolidation, the centralizing agencies through which the force of the body may work most efficiently, to the strengthening and extension of itself. It shrinks from factitious organisms suited to favor the aspirations of place-seekers. It prefers the most unmechanical, the most comprehensive, the most unsectarian plans of working. Hence, no doubt, the preference, the promptitude of our church, to co-operate with other churches in evangelical labors.

But may there not be excess even here? A denominationalism which has a right to existence, ought to have as vigorous, as useful, as efficient an existence as possible. As long as it remains pure or unsectarian, it cannot be too efficient. Such a church as ours, with numbers so large, with such intelligence, talents, and piety in its ministers and people, should not be without an organific, directing force, a force at once cohesive, concentrating and impulsive—a force whereby the activity of the whole may be directed to particular points for the achievement of particular ends. Let us think, to what would our collective force amount, if its full estimate was taken? Is there any enterpsise of holy labor to which it could not supply the adequate means, whether material, intellectual, or spiritual? Now brethren, may we have such a talent, and be under no obligations to use it?

The excellence of our denominationalism, the estimation which we ourselves have of it, requires us the more to foster it. That which in its principle is so free, so loyal, so devoted to truth, present herself as she may, so catholic, so noble, shall this be the only weak, the only uncultured denominationalism? Is its worthiness a reason for neglecting it, or a security to it against injury from neglect? Does the actual state of it, under the neglect it has received from us, prove that it is likely to thrive by means of neglect?

It is not mine to urge specific measures, or to say how fast, or how far we should proceed with them. If we are governed by our principle, we shall not be in haste. While others will work with us, we shall hardly be true to ourselves if we do not, as we have done, prefer to work with them as far as we can without compromising our distinctive interests. But some specific means, some system of agency for consolidating and energizing our church beyond any hitherto employed, ought, I must assume, to be undertaken; and without indicating measures, points may be named, to which our attention should be directed. While the thorough religious training of our people, their advancement in enlightened and solid piety, in spiritual knowledge and discernment, the rendering them strong individually in order to their becoming so collectively; while this should be diligently and patiently pursued by every appropriate means—press, pulpit, catechism, school—they should also be well instructed in the character of our denominationalism; the merits of our position when our dismemberment occurred; the nature of the novelty which has given us our name; our advantage, so far as this is concerned; our substantive orthodoxy, exempt, though we be, from bondage to names and traditions; the type of our Calvinism; the character of our authorship and literature; our place in the history of religious movements; the spirit of our ministry and churches; their unlatitudinarian liberality; their position among witnesses to the cause of evangelical truth and religion; their open, unflinching, invincible front, against every form of error and immorality; the energetic, aggressive, efficient character of our evangelism.

Again, we should nourish a denominational spirit, an *esprit du corps*, in our church, whereby, and by no other means, will it be able to combine the energy of the whole in particular enterprises. Above all, we should endeavor to augment, elevate, and strengthen our ministry, the chief means of our denominational influence, our chief concern, of course, next to the purpose of our existence—that, which being secured to the adequate extent, we shall want for nothing else; which being, on the other hand, neglected, all our undertakings will want their chariot-wheels, will be driven heavily, if they advance at all.

These, fathers and brethren, are the centres of effort, the goals to which our denominationalism should press forward, and while I am aware of a special difficulty in its way, growing out of its principle, this consciousness is more than counterbalanced by that of a fact which has, I think, the same source—a special homogeneity, the basis of a real agreement among ourselves. There is, I am confident, no extant church more capable of solidly compacting and strengthening itself than ours—none that has the materials of a more pure, dense, solid denominationalism—none, the members of which better understand, or more cordially love and confide in one another. The freeness, the flexibility of our principle to the force of evidence, by asserting its character in our history, has made us like-minded toward one another, whatever else it may have done, or not done for us. Nor should the fact that we have hitherto done so little in denominationalizing ourselves, discourage future endeavors. Our circumstances have scarcely allowed us to do more. At the date of the separation between the two schools, seventeen years ago, we were connected semi-ecclesiastically with others, with whom we expected still to co-operate as we had done, and even to be more closely associated. We have been disappointed; they have preferred separation: slowly, under the influence of changes which have been occurring from time to time, we have had to study the plan of agency proper for us: we could not anticipate what has happened; it has hindered attempts at consolidation. We are better prepared to make them now: the time for beginning them has come. We seem almost shut up to them, by the course pursued by others in regard to us; we may no longer refrain from them. At the call of Divine Providence, and in strength not our own, "let us rise and build."

IV. I have said, fourthly, that we ought to adapt our activity to the age and sphere we live in. Connected with the novelty of the manifestation which Christianity has made of itself at different periods, its new displays of life and strength, there always have been novel modifications of agency on the part of the church. The old faith and the old ordinances have been adhered to, but with new means of appliance. It was thus in the time of our Lord; it was thus with his disciples, after the opening of the new dispensation; it was thus at the revival under Luther; it has been thus at all subsequent revivals. The oldness and the newness of Christianty involve old and new forms of agency in its ministers and disciples. There are variations as to these, not only in different times, but in different places at the same time. In Germany, in France, in England, in Scotland, in this new country, the modes of religious activity have always been, as they are now, in some respects very different. They have been so, in accordance with the spirit of Christianity and apostolic example. In no church should this pliancy to circumstances, this variation of the form of activity, to suit it to the exigences of time and place, obtain more readily and completely than in our own. We are specially committed to it by the principle, the law of our denominational life. We deny our new schoolism, if amid new manifestations of the Spirit, and under new circumstances, there be not a correspondent novelty in the manner of our operations. And if the correspondence in the present case be complete—and in so far as it is incomplete, it will not be faultless—what must be this manner? As to this, one thing is clear, it will be without precedent in the history of former times; for never, and nowhere, has there been a parallel to our circumstances. In some cardinal respects, our country stands alone; and from the beginning, religion has had a bearing and an aspect here, which it has not elsewhere had. And our nationality, combining with the type of our religion, and this with that, and both with a conflux of new influences from abroad, have given us a most marked and singular status in the history of mankind. Additional to this, we experience, in common with civilized man, the force of a very novel age, before which all human and divine institutions seem to be shaking and bending. Now, if our circumstances should give fashion to our activity, ought we to look to other ages, or other countries, to supply us with its pattern? "Hence," said Dr. Owen, two hundred years ago, propounding an inference from a passage of Scripture on which he had been discoursing, "hence is the suiting of great light and great work in our days;" and he enforced this pithy inference with this no less pithy remark: "Let new light be derided, whilst men please; he will never serve the will of God in this generation, who sees not beyond the line of foregoing ages." Applying this for the regulation of our course, what will be its tenor? Will Germany, or England, or Scotland, or New England, or our own previous experience, give us its example?

Without attempting its complete delineation—a task how impracticable, amidst changes yet in progress, and new ones constantly beginning—it may be sketched, perhaps, from a few points of view. On the one hand, most certainly, our civil state, our very unique nationality, should have influence on it. This, immeasurably beyond parallel, affords us advantages for Christianizing the people, securing us perfect freedom of speech and of the press, and protecting us against interference in the exercise of this freedom, opening itself, at the same time, to appliances of Christianity—advantages not given to the apostles, the reformers, the puritans, to any of any other age or land. On the other hand, nevertheless, our activity should have a breadth, a universality of bearing, transcending all national, all local bounds. Its stamp should be that of humanity, more than that of our free, republican Americanism. The world is intensely tending to unity; the different races are flowing together, and becoming one; ideas, modes of thought, language, customs, caste, aristocracy, are ceasing to separate the children of Adam; and in this country, more than elsewhere, this restoration of the human family is advancing: all nations are here coming together and commingling; the human predominates over the national and the geographical; the links of being are becoming rather those of man with man, than those of country. If our agency is to conform itself to its sphere, will it permit itself to be stereotyped into the forms of the past; will it endure the restrictions of sect, of tribe, of tradition? Shall we preach, write, pray, labor, live, as did our predecessors, who, if they should appear again on earth, might not recognize the world which gave them birth, so changed has everything become in its condition.

In another particular, the character of the requisite agency is apparent. We shall not have to do with unlettered masses: popular education is advancing. The country abounds in schools, books, pamphlets, newspapers, lecturers; the people hear, read, think on all subjects, political, scientific, moral, religious; they are becoming familiar, they will be more and more familiar, with the objections of infidels and the difficulties of Christianity. Swift as the sun's rays is the flight of knowledge through the land.

Hence, a necessity will be upon us to make more use than we have done, of the great energies of the press; we cannot otherwise make effectual aggression on the irreligious masses, or even get access to them. We must employ abundantly a vigorous, attractive, popular, solid literature. We must have the mastery in knowledge and learning; in criticism and interpretation; in science and philosophy; in writing and book-making, as well as in eloquence and public speaking. This necessity will not abate; it will greatly increase the demand for spiritual-mindedness and self-consecration.

It has been thought that the pulpit is to have less to do; that preaching itself is to become secondary to the press. There is no probability of this. The province of preaching is distinct from every other, has a distinct and independent ground; and if every other means should attain its end and cease, this would remain, and be more than ever in demand, and more than ever productive and useful. Preaching has two purposes; one of instruction and persuasion, the other of worship—a means of faith and spiritual discernment of divine things. If for the first it were no longer needed, for the other it would be needed more. If preaching and every other agency were no longer required to make converts; if there were none left to be converted—to say to his neighbor, or brother, know the Lord, because all would know him, from the greatest to the least—there would be for this cause a larger use of the pulpit; there would be more and better preaching, and it would be more effective and useful. The supremacy among means was given to the pulpit, not for a time, but till the end of time. Its sphere is, and will remain, the upper, the upholding, the all-actuating and all-strengthening sphere. The form of preaching will change; other changes will bring on this; the mould and fashion of sermons, with everything else, will become new; but sermons, instead of ceasing or being less in demand, are, doubtless, to be both more abundant and more excellent and efficient than they have been generally in any former age. In its own sphere, the press has immeasurable power; but, like everything else, it is subordinate to the pulpit, which, in proportion to its success, it must aggrandize, stimulate, and strengthen. "I many a time say," remarks a very original author, "the writers of newspapers, pamphlets, poems, books, these are the real, working, effective church of a modern country." In one sense, they may be, perhaps, but not in a sense which implies the supersedure of preaching, without the continuance and the supremacy of which there would soon be no church, though all should be writers and book-makers, and better than the best, whether of the living or the dead.

But will not preaching, it has been asked, be less exclusively professional, less confined to an ordained ministry, more as it was in the early days of Christianity, before the clergy became a caste, a guild of priests; before the return of sacerdotalism suppressed the exercise of speaking-gifts in the laity? As to this, we ought, perhaps, to anticipate a change; indeed, a change is now taking place, and the exigences of the age seem to require that it go on. If it may but proceed without indecency and disorder, is not its consummation to be desired? "In a convert-making church," says one of the strongest and best of modern writers, "in a convert-making church, to which, after the apostolic model, believers are added daily; in such a church, neither its onward progress nor its permanence, can, in the nature of things, be provided for and secured, except by calling forth the gifts, and by allowing and favoring the services of laymen, locally connected with each single congregation. A church, which, in the spirit of rigid and arrogant adhesion to certain principles and rules, persists in refusing all such aid, and will do what it does only by means of educated and ordained ministers, must abide by the inevitable consequences; that is to say, must fail in a main article of Christian duty, and be content to sleep with them that sleep." If this be so, as a general fact, much more in the scenes which are before us. It will not be for us, certainly, to suppress lay-agency; the question as to *lay-preaching* is a delicate one, which we cannot now examine; but let not our views as to order imply that order must be at an end, when all, in the use of whatever gifts they possess, are abounding in the work of the Lord: perfect church-order requires this precisely. Then is true order kept perfectly in a church, when every gift of every individual, lawyer, physician, tradesman, artizan, male and female, is fully and regularly developed. Order is a positive thing; otherwise, who more orderly than the dead in their graves? All have not the gift of speaking; all who have it are not to exercise it in the pulpit, but exercise it they must in the service of the church, or incur a grave responsibility. "There is, one would say," says an author before cited, "there is, and ever must remain, while man has a tongue, a distinct province for speech, as well as for writing and printing." Yes, a distinct province, undoubtedly, and it is, I add, the uppermost and overruling province.

V. I mentioned as yet another object of our attention, greater regard than has been common to the end for which the church was designed, in administrative activity—measures of government and oversight. The government of the church should have paramount respect to this end, no less than should that of a state to the end of its appointment. The church and the state have different purposes. A state exists for itself, for self-wellbeing; accordingly, all procedures of government in it are carried on: a state must not interfere with the rights of other nations; incidentally its administrative measures may advance the good of mankind; but a state exists, not for benevolent ends, but for its own advantage. It would be forsaking its sphere, renouncing its proper end and character, by setting itself to the improvement of mankind, and, with reference to this, administering its affairs. If this nation should manage its finance, its army, its marine; conduct its elections, hold its assemblies, arrange its cabinet; in a word, carry on its government for the reformation of morals in Europe or elsewhere, it would mistake its mission, it would disown its character as a nation. The church, on the contrary, would be doing precisely what it was intended for, by administering its government with reference to such an end. The church exists, it is true, for its own benefit, its self-edification; but this object has reference to a further one, which, as Dr. Arnold has well said, is the putting down of moral evil, whether in itself or in the world. The kingdom of Christ, though not of the world, was for the express intent of acting on the world, as a reclaiming and reformatory instrument. It was to be intensely and ceaselessly aggressive—to conduct its government analogously to that of an ambitious state, aiming at universal empire, and pursuing, in every direction, wars of conquest. Though its weapons were not to be carnal, its battles not for, but against the objects for which nations fight, it was, in its ultimate bearings on its obstinate adversaries, to be more terrible than "an army with banners." See how she is characterized in the inspired Word: "Behold, I will make thee a new sharp-threshing instrument, having teeth: thou shalt thresh the mountains, and beat them small, and shalt make the hills as chaff: thou shalt fan them, and the wind shall carry them away, and the whirlwind shall scatter them." (Isaiah xli, 15, 16.) Taking, hence, our idea as to the design and work of the church, what a misnomer will it seem to us, to call by this name any inert or introactive corporation? A church government, which does not assume that it is to have reference, first and last, to a ceaselessly agonistic contest against moral evil, wherever it is to be found; that it is to set itself to the pulling down of the strongholds of iniquity, and bringing into captivity every thought to the obedience of Christ—to set itself to this as its appointed work, through the length and breadth of the earth—overlooks the purpose for which Christianity, with its church and all its provisions of grace and power, was intended. And know we not, fathers and brethren, that this mistake has been made, and that it is still almost universal? Among moral mysteries, this has the pre-eminence. After eighteen centuries, the world remains unsubdued, the largest part not acknowledging Christ, so much as in name, and where he is acknowledged, not a few denying him in works.

In view of this fact, some assert that the church and Christianity are failures; but failures it does not prove them to be, unless experiment as to their efficiency has been made; and can we think that this experiment has been made, when we look at the character of the business which, since the days of the first Christians, has engaged the activity of the church, and especially that of church-conventions and councils, met for administrative purposes? As to the result of experiment, there has been no failure, no possibility of one; the only failure that can be charged, is, that the experiment has not been made.

There is, let it not be overlooked, a special cause for what is so much to be deplored. The church, almost from the beginning, has been harrassed by intestine evils; its members, its ministers, in many instances, have been its chief enemies; its doctrines have been corrupted; it has been annoyed incessantly by unholy alliances with the world; it has been obliged to look narrowly to its internal state. The condition of the church has resembled that of a country, which, while foreign invasion calls for all its resources, has to carry on civil wars. But giving this fact its full force, the church's negligence of the main purpose for which it was founded, especially, and above all in its administrative functions, remains before us as a characteristic fact, throughout nearly its whole history. This, which may be well termed the summit of moral blindness and perverseness, is not always to remain. The experiment as to the efficiency of the church will at length be made. A change promising this has begun. The piety of the church is becoming more outwardly active, more combattive against evil, more missionary. The character of its administrative business, must of course become, indeed, is becoming, correspondingly different. Not the settlement of domestic disputes, the trial of appeals, the review of records, the censure and correction of violations of order, the search after, and the condemnation of heresy, the testifying against errors and irregularities ; these, however necessary and important, will not be the chief things to be attended to ; no, they will be comparatively as nothing, even as the land which the church has gained, is as nothing compared with the vast regions of heathenism, imposture, superstition and irreligion, which remain to be converted into the vineyard, the garden of God. The devising new ways and means of aggression, the conducting of itineracies and missions, the increase and improvement of the ministry, the rendering all the churches missionary institutions, and engaging all their members one way or another, in missionary work, plans for developing the resources of the church in carrying on evangelical labors, far, near, and everywhere—these, and such as these, should be the chief articles of business—the starting, points of new administrative activity and wisdom.

I have thus, fathers and brethren, presented most imperfectly and feebly, I am aware, what I take to be the outline of Ecclesiastical Prudence, the course of wisdom and expediency for us, as a religious denomination. Assuming it to be so, and that the completion of it is neccessary to our highest ecclesiastical efficiency, we cannot but feel ourselves bound to adopt it. It is an authoritative law which we may not cast away from us. We have no strength which we should not use in the service of Him whose we are. We owe to Him, the whole of our *collective* as well as individual strength. To deny this, is to assume that a church or society, as such, is not perfectly under law to Christ—an assumption generally acted on, it is true, in the corporations of earth, sacred as well as secular—but not therefore the less illicit, or the less fraught with evil. Nothing is denounced more emphatically by our Divine Master, the Lord and Judge of all, than the non-use of his gifts. Nor is this terrible severity without reason. What greater provocation of his displeasure can there be, than thus practically counting as worthless, what it cost him the sacrifice of Himself to obtain. This, it truly is, that solves the mystery of the imperfect and transcient successes, the so-called failure of Christianity. It is, altogether from this, as the judicial cause, that the agency of the Holy Spirit has been so restrained, and the world, until this day, left unevangelized.

It is not to be forgotten, nevertheless, that, as I have before said, zeal for denominational consolidation and advancement, is specially perilous to the cause of Christianity—the cause for which all churches exist. There is an aptitude in it to become sectarian, selfish, self-agrgandizing; an aptitude which, perhaps in no instance, has altogether been suppressed. If it begins pure, it is in danger of degenerating into the ambition and pride of sect, of building and glorying in a Babylon of its own, and using its strength more against other churches, than for the salvation of mankind. We may perhaps think ourselves less exposed to this peril, from the peculiararity of our principle, but we may be deceived by this very presumption. "Let him who thinks he standeth, take heed lest he fall." Our duty is plain, we must give our whole strength, our utmost collective efficiency to the cause of Christianity. We incur risks, we may, through the want of watchfulness and the deceitfulness of sin, fall into abuses; but the alternative is disloyalty to Christ, and the violation of conscience. The principle which would excuse us from the utmost effort in this case, would allow us to forbear all moral agency, because of the possibility of sinning in the exercise of it.

But, supposing our programme of activity perfect, and our activity itself unobjectionable, what then? Is our success certain? If we shun the rock of sectarian ambition, may we not still fail as to the great purpose, the goal of our denominational activity? As to this, unquestionably, we must acknowledge our dependence, our absolute self-impotence. Machinery, however perfect, cannot move without the application of the power. It is not his diligence in planting and watering that gives the husbandman his increase. The bodies in the prophet's valley of vision, though exquisitely organized, remained lifeless until they were breathed upon by breath from the four winds. In the present case, above every other, the result is not the product of finite forces, however great or well-directed—not of might, or of power, but of the Spirit of the Lord of Hosts. And as to the co-operation of this Spirit, there is at least one condition of its being granted: the spirit of grace and of supplication must be poured upon us: "I will be inquired of by the house of Israel to do it for them." This is indispensable; talents, gifts, labors, are no substitutes for it; and if it be wanting, all else will be of small avail. And in regard to this, at least, is there not a deficiency? Amidst all the machinery of the times, and all that has been done, and is being done by means of it, is not that one thing absent, without which everything else is unavailing—even as soil, seed and tending can produce nothing when the heavens are shut up, so that there is no rain or dew? Among the new measures and movements of this most remarkable age, has prayer in the church the prominence which it has in the Scriptures, as an appointed means of spreading the gospel through the world? The guarantee of success in this work is not in our advantages, or in any use we may make of them. The way of God, in the sphere of his saving power, has not been after the method of natural processes, or in the sequence of secondary and dependent causes. Not thus, but strikingly the opposite, has been His way, in this supernatural sphere of His agency: While he has wrought in it by a continual influence, and through stated means, he has ever and anon asserted the supernatural character of his operation, by supernatural phenomena—by extraordinary manifestations of his Spirit at special seasons of mercy.

It is not given to us to anticipate with assurance, the coming times and seasons—to bind or loose the influences of the Eternal Spirit. We have no absolute knowledge, therefore, as to what is predestined for us; but we know as much as we should know: We have no cause for despondence at the prospect before us. Our motives could not be stronger or our encouragement greater. We have passed through the wilderness-state of our church: we stand to-day on the shores of Jordan, and O what a land of promise is opened to us! and what clearer warrant, what more imperative command, could we have to take possession of it in the name of the Lord! What animation to effort—greater than has been heretofore given to any church—in our sphere, in the age, in the state of the world! and then what advantages, also! All parts of the earth accessible; the distance to its very ends virtually only a few miles; the subtilest and strongest forces of nature subsidized as means of operation: Other denominations, too, in the advance; effort, wherever made, crowned with success—this is one view, and it could not be brighter. There is another, of a different character, not less exciting: The enemy, like a flood, is spreading over the length and breadth of the land, compassing the camp of the saints, filling every place with the deadly miasma of his delusions, wielding the enginery of the age, material and spiritual, against Christian truth and piety, and the scenes of his proudest triumphs here directly before our eyes.

Such are the circumstances in which our church finds itself, at this transition stage of its career. Detatched from incongenial associations which we did not wish to disturb, disappointing hopes and fears, falsifying predictions as to our permanence, surmounting many disadvantages and obstacles to our progress, we have grown into comparative strength and magnitude, and are in a position of great interest and animation: I need not say that our situation and circumstances are a call to us from God, a loud and imperative call, to make full proof of whatever we may have of talent or advantages, for the furtherance of the cause of Christ. And if we cannot fully obey this call without applying our collective strength—without a complete development and concentration of our denominational force—then the obligation to do this is upon us, and we must not throw it off; we are shut up to the discharge of it by an absolute necessity, from which there is no escape, but by a violation of palpable duty. Perils may be incidental to our undertaking. We do not claim to be better than others. If our denominationalism be better, or the best, our heart may deceive us; ere we are aware we may bind ourselves, as others have done, in the cords of sectarianism, and enter into a strife to be great among the sects, and cease contending for the advancement of Christianity, except as a means of our own advancement. There is a possibility of this, and we may be wanting in the vigilance necessary to its not becoming a reality. Still no choice is left us; if there is risk in advancing, it is the risk of unnecessary inadvertance or wilful perverseness: at any rate, the alternative is rebellion.

Other denominations will not blame us: they have set us an example, and are blamable themselves, if it be not right for us to imitate it. Moreover, what else can we do? They have compelled us to this course. It is not we who have ceased to co-operate with them; it is they who have preferred to work by themselves. They are industriously building themselves up in denominational strength; shall we be committing an offence, if we walk in their footsteps? No; we shall thus command their regard, and take the surest way to secure the return of a more comprehensive activity.

Fathers and brethren, how intense, how profound, the interest of the meeting which we are to hold in this place! How solemn the assembly, in which seventeen hundred churches are to consult and act together, in the name of Christ, and for the cause of Christ, the cause for which he died on the cross, arose from the dead, ascended the throne of the world, and administers the government of God! How great, how sublime, the representative activity, in which we are to be engaged, as the delegates and organs of these churches! In virtue of his own wisdom or holiness, which of us is sufficient for the part he has to perform in this sacred convocation? For a just discernment of the character and relations of the work we are to do, for the state of heart, the spiritual understanding, the motives, the views, the ends which should control us, how incompetent are we all, apart from the illuminating and gracious unction of the Holy One! Nay, what a special baptism of the Spirit do we need, in order to be furnished as we should be for the business with which we have been intrusted by the churches we represent? Can we imagine any measure of spiritual discernment, any vividness and freshness of spiritual views, any exercises of sanctity, too great for the functions we have to discharge? If, under a sudden illapse of the Eternal Spirit, we should be moved, as the disciples were at first, should we have a needless, wasteful measure of His influence? If the Blessed Spirit should actually fall upon us with such fullness of power and light, ought we to receive the visitation with a misgiving mind? we, above all, who, by our very title, are marked and committed as expectants of novelties like this? There are, doubtless, to be divine interventions scarcely less novel, less wonderful, than that which signalized the instalment of the new dispensation. Our hope of the great triumph of the gospel, rests on them as its only adequate ground. Not our arrangements, not our labors, not the combined labors of all the churches, not the great advantages of the times—no, fathers and brethren, no—but mighty manifestations of the Spirit: these, these are to accomplish the redemption and renovation of the world. And one thing more, these manifestations do not come when men are expecting them; they come in an hour we know not of. "In every instance," says a profound observer, "the return of truth and piety has been a bright and sudden visitation from on high, as in the thickest gloom of the night." It was all of a sudden, that the sound from heaven, as of a rushing mighty wind, was heard by the first disciples; and was not this according to the word of the holy prophet: "The Lord whom ye seek shall suddenly come unto His temple." What if He should suddenly reveal himself, in the midst of our assembly? What if we should enter upon the business before us with impressions of His presence, new and fresh as those imparted by the pentecostal baptism! If we have expected no such manner of beginning, neither did the disciples expect what came to pass on the morning of the day of Pentecost. Not our expectations, not our prayers, but His own purpose and the exigences of His cause, are the measure and the reason of the outpouring of the Spirit from on high.

www.ingramcontent.com/pod-product-compliance
Lightning Source LLC
LaVergne TN
LVHW011139110826
845150LV00008B/2418
9781418193485